INTERVENTIONS IN CASES OF BULLYING IN SCHOOLS

A TRAINING MANUAL FOR TEACHERS AND COUNSELLORS

DR KEN RIGBY OAM

© 2023 Kenneth Rigby

All rights reserved. No part of this book may be reproduced or transmitted in any form or by any means, electronic or mechanical, including photocopying, recording or by any information storage and retrieval system, without prior permission in writing from the publisher.

Published in 2023 by Amba Press, Melbourne, Australia.
www.ambapress.com.au

Previously published in 2023 by Hawker Brownlow Education.
This edition replaces all previous editions.

ISBN: 9781923116048 (pbk)
ISBN: 9781923116055 (ebk)

Images on pages 26–27 provided by Allan Adams, used with permission.

Images on the cover and pages i, 9, 16, 20 and 23 provided by Simon Kneebone, used with permission.

Terms of use for this publication

This work is copyright. With one exception detailed below, all rights are reserved. Apart from fair dealings for the purposes of study, research, criticism or review, or as permitted under the Copyright Act 1968 (Cth), no part should be reproduced, transmitted, communicated or recorded, in any form or by any means, without the prior written permission of the copyright owner.

Blackline master pages

You may be able to photocopy content within this work beyond your rights under the Copyright Act 1968 (Cth) provided that:
1. Pages are marked as photocopiable, AND
2. You are the purchaser of this publication.

A catalogue record for this book is available from the National Library of Australia.

TABLE OF CONTENTS

About the author ... v
1. Introduction ... 1
2. Bullying defined ... 4
3. How this book may be used by schools ... 5
4. List of methods of intervention ... 6
5. Conducting workshops ... 7
6. The traditional disciplinary approach ... 8
7. Strengthening the victim ... 10
8. Mediation ... 17
9. Restorative practice ... 19
10. Support group method ... 22
11. The method of shared concern ... 25
12. Other intervention methods ... 32
    a. Solution-focused brief therapy (SFBT)
    b. School tribunals or bully courts
    c. Motivational interviewing
13. Group bullying and bullying by individual students ... 34
14. Cyberbullying ... 35
15. Choosing the best methods ... 36
16. Exercise on selecting a method ... 38
17. Interviewing students involved in bullying ... 40
18. The school anti-bullying policy and its relationship with dealing with cases of bullying ... 43

Appendix A: Outcomes ... 45
Appendix B: Recording form ... 46
References and recommendations ... 50

ABOUT THE AUTHOR

Dr Ken Rigby OAM was born in England in 1932 and served for two years in the Royal Navy before acquiring an honours degree in economics from the University of London and a teaching diploma from the University of Leicester. For ten years Dr Rigby was employed as a teacher, first in England and then in Australia, where he was naturalised. Since 1969 he has been a member of the staff of the University of South Australia, where he taught psychology and research methods and is currently an adjunct professor. In 1977 he was awarded a PhD in psychology by the University of Adelaide.

Dr Rigby is the author of over a hundred research articles in peer-reviewed journals and eleven books on bullying in schools, published by Routledge, Blackwell and Wiley among others. He has served as advisor on issues relating to school bullying to three Australian state education departments and has been invited to present at numerous conferences and workshops in Australia, New Zealand, Europe, Africa, Asia and North America. For service to education and his work in promoting the wellbeing of young people he was awarded a Medal of the Order of Australia in 2020.

1. INTRODUCTION

This book is a plan for a series of school workshops on intervening in cases of identified bullying. It is not intended as a substitute for policy development and preventive programs delivered in classrooms, such as social and emotional learning (SEL), but rather as a necessary supplement for addressing actual cases of bullying.

As teachers are aware, schools normally give a great deal of attention to providing a positive school ethos and promoting positive relationships between members of the school community, including staff, students and parents. Much has been written about what schools can do to prevent bullying (see Rigby, 2007, 2021b; Wicking & Rigby, 2021; Salmivalli et al., 2005). When this is achieved, bullying is less likely to occur. However, even in the best run schools, cases of bullying continue to arise and must be addressed.

It is worth reminding ourselves of why action is needed. There is now a mountain of evidence confirming that if a child is continually bullied at school, the effects on their wellbeing are often serious and sometimes long-lasting. These include prolonged anxiety in social situations, depression, absences from school and workplaces, and the inability to form positive relationships and succeed occupationally (see Rigby, 2003). A second reason for action, not so widely acknowledged, is the harm that can be done to a school and its teachers when no appropriate action is taken to deal with the bullying and the school is deemed culpable.

As an expert witness in cases of bullying where legal action is taken against a school, most commonly by a parent of a bullied child, I am keenly aware of the shock and dismay schools experience when faced with such a situation. The school is always asked to say what they did and did not do about an alleged case of bullying, and why. The school is also asked to provide a copy of the anti-bullying policy operating at the time of the incident or incidents. Records of what the school actually did, who was involved and the outcomes of these interventions are also requested. When a school is found to be seriously at fault, large fines are commonly imposed; the school's reputation is tarnished; and individual staff members may experience career setbacks. Worse still, staff members may have to live with the belief that if they had acted otherwise the victimised child would not have suffered so badly.

This is not to say that schools can invariably stop cases of bullying from continuing. In most cases the bullying continues – and in some cases it actually increases! A summary of available evidence on the effects of case interventions in Australia, England, Germany, Finland, the Netherlands and the United States is compiled in Appendix A (page 45), and an extensive meta-analysis of reported outcomes for some interventions is given by Ttofi and Farrington (2011).

The first thing we should bear in mind is that resolving cases of bullying has repeatedly been shown to be difficult, often unsuccessful and sometimes counterproductive. Indeed, the evidence from a number of countries, based on student reports, indicates that among students who have gone to teachers for help, most interventions are not entirely successful in getting the bullying stopped. Both teachers and school counsellors differ among themselves on what course of action should be taken (see Bauman et al., 2008). The common response is to apply what has been called the *traditional disciplinary approach*; that is, to identify the bully or bullies and apply sanctions or punishment (Sherer & Nickerson, 2010). This approach is sometimes appropriate and effective, but in a very large number of cases, alternative or supplementary approaches have been found to be much more successful in getting the bullying to stop (see Thompson & Smith, 2011; Rigby & Johnson, 2016). Unfortunately, teachers are often unaware of alternative methods or lack the training or confidence to use them.

The purpose of this book is to provide information about a range of methods and offer the means by which they can be understood and used appropriately. It emphatically does not seek to replace the expertise and professional judgement of teachers based upon their personal, day-to-day experiences of observing and interacting with students. Rather, it provides a rationale (which must be discussed) for taking one course of action rather than another in response to a case of bullying. It provides a considered basis for making judgements and carrying out actions that can over time result in a substantial reduction of bullying in schools and a corresponding increase in the wellbeing of students, especially of those for whom bullying and the fear of bullying is a recurring nightmare.

The content of this book is largely based on *Bullying Interventions in Schools: Six Basic Methods*, which I first published in 2010. The role-plays and exercises provided have been extensively workshopped in many Australian schools and also internationally over the last ten years.

This book provides concise descriptions of methods of intervention in actual cases of bullying and the rationales for employing them. Further, it provides a series of exercises and role-plays designed to assist teachers in carrying out each method of intervention. It is not proposed that any single method is appropriate for dealing with all forms of bullying. Rather, it is suggested that particular methods or combinations of methods can be applied selectively according to the nature of the bullying. Teachers and counsellors need to become aware of each of the intervention methods and how they can be implemented – and then discuss their pros and cons, and under what circumstances they may be applied.

I should add that, in detailing the practical aspects of these six methods, I am not dismissing the value and potential effectiveness of other approaches in dealing with cases of bullying, some of which appear to be intuitive, depend on the unique relationship between teacher and student, or are yet to be thoroughly evaluated. In this book I will touch on several of these additional approaches, and I encourage other educators to extend the array of resources available to teachers dealing with the seemingly intractable problem of bullying. I have also provided a means by which a school can systematically record and evaluate the methods that it uses to deal with cases of bullying (see Appendix B, pages 46–49). Schools can then decide what methods work best for them.

Finally, although this book was written for professional learning in schools, its use may be extended for pre-service teacher education.

2. BULLYING DEFINED

Teachers know what bullying is, at least as well as I do. However, when the word *bullying* is paired with *intervention* it is sometimes confused with lots of other things that may lead a teacher to intervene, such as students disrupting a lesson, fighting or breaking a school rule. Hence, we must begin with identifying what bullying is and what it is not.

A common definition contains these three elements:
1. a desire to hurt or dominate someone.
2. acting repeatedly to do so.
3. causing significant harm to the person targeted, physically or emotionally.

It is also necessary to specify that bullying is *not* the same thing as fighting or quarrelling between people of similar power or status. Rather, it occurs in situations in which targeted persons are unable or unwilling to defend themselves.

Bullying can, as we know, take different forms, including physical assault, verbal aggression, exclusion and cyber abuse. It may be perpetrated by individuals acting alone or by groups of students supporting each other.

Bullying is now universally recognised as a major source of distress among students and seriously affects educational outcomes, wellbeing and mental health. For a comprehensive, research-based account of school bullying, see Smith (2014).

Teachers have a duty of care to do what they can to prevent bullying from happening in a school and to intervene when bullying is identified.

3. How this book may be used by schools

- Decide on how much time can be allocated for conducting training sessions on bullying interventions with staff. At least two or three sessions of approximately one hour are needed.
- Given time constraints, it may be decided that only exercises and role-plays that are of greatest interest are to be undertaken during the sessions.
- Ensure that at the end of each role-play the participants are debriefed, the relevant method is discussed, and views on the pros and cons of the method, as well as areas of application, are considered.
- Allow time for the exercise on selecting a method (page 38) and discuss the answers that are given.
- After every case you come across and intervention you employ, describe what actions were taken using the recording form in Appendix B (pages 46–49).
- Carefully monitor what happens over the next few weeks and complete the record sheet. This should include meetings with the bully, the victim and, if justified, other students, teachers and parents.
- Submit the record sheet to the principal of the school or other nominee.
- After they have had the opportunity to use one or more of the methods in dealing with cases of bullying, arrange to meet again with the staff to re-appraise the interventions.
- Periodically review the information from the combined record sheets and arrange for a report based on the feedback that has been received to be written and then shared with all staff.
- It is suggested that workshop participants, and especially designated leaders, become acquainted with some of the extensive literature on bullying in schools prior to any workshops being conducted. Consult the references given on pages 50–52, noting the asterisked resources. It is recommended that the leader should access and read one or more of them, as well as this book, in preparing for workshops.

4. LIST OF METHODS OF INTERVENTION

Six basic methods of intervention have been identified (Rigby, 2010). The method chosen should be the one considered most suitable for a given case, taking into account the nature and severity of the bullying and whether two or more students are involved. In some cases, a combination of methods may be justified.

The six basic methods are:
1. the traditional disciplinary approach
2. strengthening the victim
3. mediation
4. restorative practice
5. the support group method
6. the method of shared concern.

In addition, three other methods have been described, but more briefly. These are:
1. solution-focused brief therapy (SFBT)
2. school tribunals or bully courts
3. motivational interviewing.

In the following pages each method is described with suggestions for use. Discuss each one of them.

You may decide, given time constraints, that you will role-play only a selection of these methods. If this is the case, I suggest that you select strengthening the victim (page 10), which can be fun as well as useful, and the method of shared concern (page 25), which can be demanding, but once grasped and applied can be extremely effective, as evaluations have shown. But make sure that you have discussed each one of them during the workshop. Pause between role-plays to debrief and discuss the practicality and scope of applying the method with students. Schools – and teachers – differ according to what they find acceptable and useful.

5. CONDUCTING WORKSHOPS

When conducting workshops on bullying interventions, it is suggested that copies of this book be provided to each group member at the beginning of the first meeting. It should be explained that the meetings are primarily concerned about helping teachers to become familiar with a range of different intervention methods being used in some schools and to evaluate their possible use. This will involve selected role-plays and discussions based on questions that are provided.

In selecting or preparing a venue for workshops, make sure that there is sufficient space for everyone in the group to take part in these role plays with a partner from time to time.

In conducting any of the selected role-plays it is suggested that you have a particular case in mind. Here is an example you may use, but feel free to make one up if you prefer.

> A thirteen-year-old student is being repeatedly teased and called unpleasant names by another, more powerful student who has successfully persuaded other students to avoid the targeted person as much as possible.
>
> There is also evidence that the targeted student has been receiving threatening and abusive text messages instigated by the person who has been identified as 'the bully'.
>
> As a result, the victim of this behaviour is feeling angry, miserable and often isolated.
>
> What has been happening has come to the attention of the school and a teacher or counsellor has undertaken to deal with this case.

A note about the use of terms

In this book the term *bully*, or *suspected bully*, is used to describe a person who has perpetrated or is thought to have perpetrated bullying. The term *victim*, or *target*, is used to describe the person who has been bullied. It is recognised that such language runs the risk of encouraging labelling, especially if the words are used to imply that the individuals so described are fixed in their behaviour and unable to change. However, in the interest of providing clear instructions in the workshops, the disputed terminology is employed alongside an injunction that such language is best avoided in talking with or about particular individuals.

6. THE TRADITIONAL DISCIPLINARY APPROACH

The traditional disciplinary approach is the most commonly employed method of bullying intervention in most countries. It involves the use of a brief interview with the suspected perpetrator of the bullying – sometimes, but not always, with the victim or others as well. The rationale is that bullying will cease if an appropriate sanction is applied and the outcomes are then monitored.

ROLE-PLAY OF THE TRADITIONAL DISCIPLINARY APPROACH

1. Familiarise yourself with the case on page 7 or an invented case.
2. Work in pairs. Decide who will be the practitioner and who will be the bully. (A common method of deciding is giving the individual who has the next birthday the role of practitioner.)
3. The practitioner should follow the instructions given next. (The bully should close the book and *not* be reading the following when the interview is being conducted.) The whole interview should be matter-of-fact and last for five minutes or so.

Instructions for the practitioner

1. Assume the interaction is private, rather than public with others watching.
2. Begin by making it clear that you know what has been happening, that it constitutes bullying, and that it is 'completely unacceptable in this school'. Don't get into arguments about what has been happening. It is assumed that the facts are clear.
3. Ask the student what they have to say about it, but do not accept any excuses.
4. Point out that there are school rules against such behaviour in accordance with the school's anti-bullying policy – and there are consequences for students who engage in bullying others.
5. State the nature of the sanctions that are to be applied in *this* case. (These may include detentions, temporary loss of privileges, community service, meetings with parents, suspensions or exclusion – decide on what you think is appropriate.)

6. Stress what will happen next if the bullying continues, and that the bully's behaviour will be continually observed.

Discussion questions

- How did the bully feel about how they were treated by the practitioner? What effect is this likely to have on:
   a. their subsequent behaviour?
   b. their relationship with the practitioner?
- How did the practitioners see themselves in applying this approach? Which of the two scenarios illustrated in figure 1, A or B, seemed more like them in manner?

FIGURE 1: Disciplining the bully – two approaches

- Do you think this disciplinary approach is ever justified? If so, under what circumstances?

Differences of opinion are likely to occur among participants – and nobody should be accused of having the 'wrong' view. You might like to consider how a disciplinary method can be handled best to avoid negative outcomes.

Further reading

For further suggestions on how sanctions or consequences may be imposed, see the following:

Gordon, S. (2020, September 23). How to discipline bullies at school. *Verywell Family*. www.verywellfamily.com/guidelines-for-disciplining-bullies-at-school-460745

7. STRENGTHENING THE VICTIM

It is often thought that bullying could be prevented or reduced if the victim could only develop appropriate social skills for dealing with a recurrent bullying situation.

Teachers and counsellors report that they sometimes encourage students to 'stand up for themselves'. In some cases they go further and personally help students to develop useful and appropriate social skills. One of these is involves the use of a strategy called *fogging*.

This technique generally seeks to avoid direct confrontation on the part of the victim with the bully, who is typically more powerful. The aim of the victim is to learn how to respond effectively without showing discomfort or distress, and without responding aggressively as doing so is often counterproductive. Hopefully, the bully will fail to obtain any satisfaction from the bullying and give up!

ROLE-PLAY OF STRENGTHENING THE VICTIM

The following exercise is intended to help you get a feel for how the interaction between a bully and a victim *might* go if the victim understands the method well and is able to apply it.

For the role-play you need first to decide who will play the role of the target of bullying and who will play the role of the bully. On the next pages there are two scripts: one is for the bully and one is for the target, who has learned the 'fogging' way of dealing with verbal bullying. Each of you has a different script. When role-playing you must stand up facing each other.

Script for the bully

Your role is to make a number of statements, as given below, designed to ridicule and upset the target. You do *not* have access to what the target will say. In this role-play you do *not* threaten violence.

Spend a little while getting familiar with what you have to say.

After making your statement, listen briefly (without comment) to the target's response, then move on to your next statement.

> ***Bully: You have a great big nose.***
>
> *Target:*
>
> ***Bully: It looks like a beak.***
>
> *Target:*
>
> ***Bully: You are the ugliest kid in the school.***
>
> *Target:*
>
> ***Bully: You are wearing pov shoes. (If you wish, substitute different trendy item of clothing at your school.)***
>
> *Target:*
>
> ***Bully: You must be stupid to keep agreeing with me.***
>
> *Target:*
>
> ***Bully: You keep saying 'that's true'.***
>
> *Target:*

INTERVENTIONS IN CASES OF BULLYING IN SCHOOLS

In the next part of this exercise the target will respond and ask you a question or make an observation, to which you should respond quite briefly and pass on to the next statement.

> ***Bully: You are such an idiot.***
> *Target:* ....
>
> ***Bully: Everybody hates you.***
> *Target:* ....
>
> ***Bully: All those kids in the library are nerds.***
> *Target:* ....
>
> ***Bully: You have no friends.***
> *Target:* ....

7. Strengthening the victim

Script for the target *only*

In this script you will be responding to what the 'bully' says. Note that the bully does *not* have access to your replies! When the bully makes a statement (as in the script) look the bully in the eye and give your response calmly, nonchalantly, without hostility.

Bully: You have a great big nose.

Target: True, it is large.

Bully: It looks like a beak.

Target: True, it does stand out.

Bully: You are the ugliest kid in the school.

Target: That's your opinion.

Bully: You are wearing pov shoes. (The bully may substitute another trendy item of clothing, but your response can be the same.)

Target: You are not wrong.

Bully: You must be stupid to keep agreeing with me.

Target: That's true. (Say this without sarcasm – this is not intended to 'take the bully down', but may make the bully think.)

Bully: You keep saying 'that's true'.

Target: That's true.

In the next part of the exercise the 'target' replies with a question but doesn't get into an argument.

Bully: You are such an idiot.

Target: Why do you think so? (Wait for the answer. Don't argue. Simply shrug it off.)

Bully: Everybody hates you.

Target: That's interesting. Why do you think that? (Listen but don't get drawn in.)

Bully: You are always in the library at lunch time.

Target: That's right. Why does that concern you? (Wait. The focus can now be on the bully who may struggle to verbalise a concern. Show non-verbally you are not bothered by what they think or say.)

Bully: All those kids in the library are nerds.

Target: It may seem like that to you.

Bully: You have no friends.

Target: That's what you think. (Walk away with an air of calm indifference.)

Discussion questions

1. How did people playing the bully feel about the interaction?
2. On reflection, did the target feel that the method as applied by victims could work? Modifications of the procedure may be suggested.
3. Under what circumstances (if any) could this technique be learned and used by a student?
4. Under what circumstances do you think it should not be used?
5. Are there any other considerations that might arise (for example, parent responses)? If so, how they might be handled?

Tips

Here are some tips on working with targeted students to help them respond better to verbal bullying.

- Keep in mind that you are not trying to tell the victim what to say. It is not a matter of teaching a victim a particular script. The script you have been using is to help you to get a sense of the method. What the target may actually say or do is to be worked out with the practitioner and must be something that the victim has suggested and is comfortable with.
- Never tell the victim how they ought to respond to a bully. Rather, offer your help and, if accepted, suggest how things might be improved.
- Start by finding out about how the target has been bullied and how they have responded. Listen carefully – without jumping in to tell them what to do.
- In some cases, you may decide that a direct intervention with the bully is also needed. This is more likely in cases of severe bullying or group bullying, or where it is unrealistic to expect the target to resolve the problem, whatever the training provided.
- Appraise the situation to determine whether you think the particular target could really benefit from learning the method.
- It is crucial to win the confidence and trust of the target.
- Stress the importance of self-control and keeping calm. (Acknowledge that this can be really difficult when you feel threatened and suggest ways of doing so).
- Bear in mind that getting the victim to adopt a more confident posture in interactions with the bully can help. Figure 2 (page 16) may help you to make suggestions.

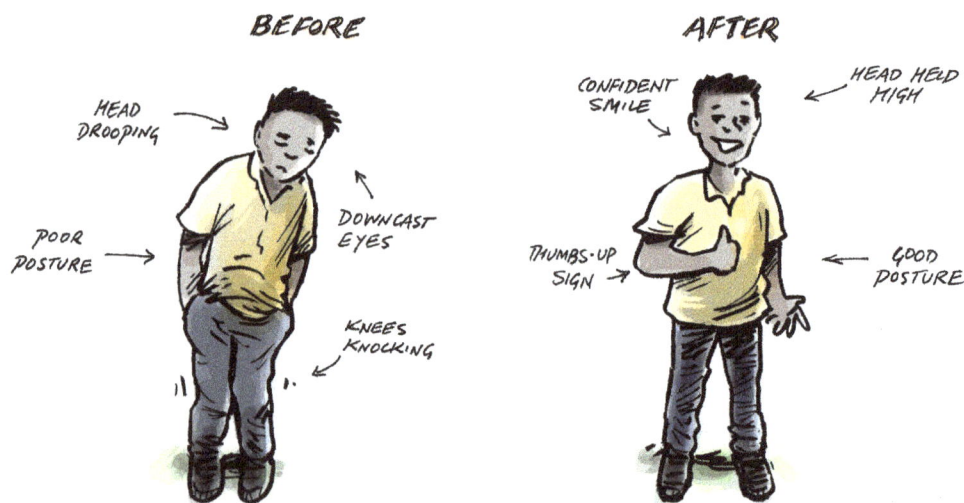

FIGURE 2: Before and after training in positive posture

- You might rehearse with the target what might be said in reply to the bully, paying attention to body posture, in a simple role-play.
- *Do not* suggest that the target is at fault, nor that the method will *definitely* work – only that it *can* work and is worth trying.
- Be prepared for several meetings to coach the student and importantly to monitor progress.

Further reading

This popular book by an Australian psychologist provides copious examples of how vulnerable students may employ effective verbal skills in resisting bullying (bear in mind that responses that are sarcastic and designed to hurt the bully can be counterproductive):

Field, E. M. (2003). *Bully Busting: How to Help Children Deal with Teasing and Bullying*. Finch Publishing.

A good description with examples of 'fogging' responses can be found here:

Girls Guide to End Bullying. (2012). Understanding fogging. *Girls Guide to End Bullying*. http://girlsguidetoendbullying.org/pdf/Understanding_Fogging.pdf

8. MEDIATION

Mediation can occur when two students agree to seek help from a mediator, a teacher or trained peer mediator to resolve an issue that is causing conflict and possibly bullying behaviour.

This method can be used when the students in conflict voluntarily – *without* any compulsion – opt to seek the help of a mediator. The method is *not* the same as arbitration, which involves those in conflict abiding by a third-party judgement.

Mediation may be practised by school counsellors, teachers or trained peer mediators only in cases of conflict in which *both or all parties* would like to see their differences resolved and the conflict stopped.

Finally, mediation can become feasible in the last stage of the method of shared concern (page 25) when students who have bullied someone express a readiness to work with the person that they have bullied to reach an agreed resolution.

ROLE-PLAY OF MEDIATION

This role-play can be carried out in groups of three: the teacher or peer mediator and the two students seated facing each other as in figure 3.

FIGURE 3: Mediation between students in conflict

Source: Murphy and Lewers (2000, p. 61)
© Curriculum Corporation. Reproduced with permission.

The presenting case can be the one used earlier (page 7) or, if you wish, one that you make up – perhaps one that has come to your attention at your school.

1. The mediator asks each of the students in turn to explain the situation as they see it.
2. The other student is required to listen without interrupting and, at the end, to summarise what has been said – to the satisfaction of the speaker.
3. Each is then asked to make suggestions as to how the issue might be resolved. The mediator records each suggestion without unnecessary comment.
4. Each suggestion is listed, then examined and discussed to discover one that they agree will help resolve the conflict.

Discussion questions

Whether mediation has been role-played or not, it can be useful to discuss the following questions:

- Under what circumstances (if any) do you think the method can be effectively used when bullying occurs?
- Do you think students can be trained to practise as mediators to resolve student conflicts including bullying? If so, at what age?
- Are you in favour of its use at your school? By teachers? By counsellors? By trained students?

Further reading

Cohen, R. (2005). *Students Resolving Conflict: Peer Mediation in Schools*. Good Year Books.

9. RESTORATIVE PRACTICE

Restorative practice is designed to restore damaged relationships between individuals or groups. They require that the offender or bully acknowledges wrongdoing and the harm they have caused, and then act restoratively: for example, through an apology and by taking positive action. Ideally, this method should be introduced and explained by a person who has had some experience in successfully applying the method with students.

Most commonly, this approach is used when *one* student has been identified as bullying one other student who wishes the bullying to be stopped. (Less commonly it may be used with more than two participants as at a community conference at which the 'offender(s)' and 'target(s)' meet together with other interested parties, such as parents.)

At such meetings the bully – sometimes called the *offender* – is confronted by the practitioner in the presence of the victim, who also attends the meeting. Often these students, and sometimes others, have been seen earlier by the practitioner in the course of obtaining reliable information about the bullying and to get a better understanding of those involved. They may be asked the following questions (illustrated in figure 4, page 20):

1. What happened?
2. What were you thinking about at the time?
3. What have your thoughts been towards what happened?
4. Who do you think has been affected by your actions? In what way were they affected?
5. What do you need to do now to make things right?

RESTORATIVE PRACTICE IN SCHOOLS

1. WHAT HAPPENED?

2. WHAT WERE YOU THINKING ABOUT AT THE TIME?

3. WHAT HAVE YOUR THOUGHTS BEEN TOWARDS WHAT HAPPENED?

4. WHO DO YOU THINK HAS BEEN AFFECTED BY YOUR ACTIONS? IN WHAT WAY WERE THEY AFFECTED

5. WHAT DO YOU NEED TO DO NOW TO MAKE THINGS RIGHT?

FIGURE 4: Examples of what teachers may ask of students who have engaged in bullying, prior to a meeting involving a victim

Subsequently a meeting is called to include the bully or bullies and the victim (see 'Role-play of restorative practice' for the procedure). The bully is then expected to appreciate the harm their actions have caused and to indicate to the victim what they are prepared to do to restore the damaged relationship: for example, by apologising and committing to acting positively in future. Although it likely that the bullies will experience some shame in reflecting on their actions, care should be taken to avoid their feeling stigmatised and personally unacceptable to others. According to some practitioners of this method, some sanctions may be applied.

Role-play of restorative practice

When conducting this role-play, refer again to the sample case of bullying given on page 7. Three people are needed for this exercise: the teacher or counsellor, the bully and the victim. Assume that the bully has already acknowledged what they have been doing and is prepared to go over what has happened.

1. In the presence of the victim, the bully is asked several questions. The aim is to get the bully to appreciate that they have behaved wrongly and need to act restoratively:
   - What happened?
   - What were you thinking of at the time?
   - What have you thought about since?
   - Who has been affected by what you have done? In what way?
2. Switch now to the victim and ask:
   - What did you think when you realised what had happened?
   - What have you thought about since?
   - What impact has it had on you and on others?
   - What do you need to do to put things right?
   - What do you think needs to happen to make things right?
3. Next, it is back to the bully:
   - What do you think *you* need to do to make things right?
   - How can we make sure this doesn't happen again?

Discussion questions

- How did the bully feel about the intervention? In particular, did the bully feel stigmatised or alienated? Alternatively, did they feel treated with respect and subsequently expect to be accepted by the school?
- How did the victim feel? Did the apology and the promised actions by the bully strike the victim as sincere and likely to resolve the issue?
- Under what circumstances might this method be applied?

Further reading

The following resource is written by Australian practitioners and trainers in the use of the method, based on two decades of working closely with schools:

Thorsborne, M., & Vinegrad, D. (2006). *Restorative Practice and the Management of Bullying: Rethinking Behaviour Management*. Inyahead Press.

10. SUPPORT GROUP METHOD

This is a method of intervention that was designed and developed by Barbara Maines and George Robinson in the 1990s and is considered to be a very effective method for intervening in cases of group bullying.

There are seven steps in the method, beginning with an interview with the victim, then holding a meeting with a group of students including both the bullies and other students (but not the victim), and ending with meetings with the individuals who have taken part in the application of the method.

Step 1: Talking with the victim

The practitioner meets with the victim to establish the impact that the bullying has had. The victim is encouraged to provide a detailed and graphic account of the distress that they have experienced. This may take the form of a piece of writing or a drawing that expresses how the student has been affected. The victim is asked to identify the bullies. Importantly, assurance is given that *no-one* will be punished.

Step 2: Convening a group meeting

This meeting includes the students who have been identified as those engaging in the bullying, and also some other students who are selected by the practitioner because they are expected to be helpful in bringing about a positive outcome. The victim is *not* required to be present. Generally, the group size is between five and eight students. Figure 5 indicates a possible arrangement of participants.

Note that nothing is done to identify the bullies at this meeting. Everyone is equally valued.

Step 3: Explaining the problem

The practitioner draws attention to the problem and especially to the distress that the victim is experiencing, using evidence provided by the victim. Specific incidents are not described and *no accusations* are made.

Step 4: Promoting shared responsibility

It is made clear that no-one is going to be punished, that the group has been convened to help solve the problem, and that everyone has a responsibility to improve the situation.

10. Support group method

FIGURE 5: A meeting at which the support group method is being applied

Step 5: Asking for ideas

The practitioner asks each member in turn for suggestions about how things can be made better for the victim. This includes both the bullies and the victim supporters.

Each person present is asked to make a personal statement on what they will do to help.

Step 6: Leaving it up to them

Having explained the situation, the practitioner passes responsibility for the problem over to the group, thanks them for their support and indicates that there will be further meetings with each of the students to see how things are going. The students are then left to continue the discussion if they want to do so, uninfluenced by the teacher. In this way they are more likely to 'own' what they said they would do.

Step 7: Final meetings

A week or so later the practitioner meets with members of the group individually to ascertain progress. The victim is also interviewed as part of the monitoring process.

ROLE-PLAY OF THE SUPPORT GROUP METHOD

It is suggested that a first role-play could involve the practitioner of the method and a student who it is believed has been bullied. Remember the purpose of the meeting is:

    a. to offer support to the victim

    b. to find out in detail how they have been affected by the bullying.

Keep in mind that this information is to be shared later with the students (bullies and victim supporters) at a meeting to be convened.

A second role-play could involve those who have bullied the victim (say two or three people) and those who have been invited by the practitioner to be present to take part at the meeting (say 3–5 people). The targeted student or victim should *not* be present.

If either or both these role-plays are undertaken, obtain feedback on how the actors felt about their involvement.

Discussion questions

- Under what circumstances might this method be used or not used?
- What difficulties might the practitioner experience in conducting the group meeting – and how might they be overcome?

Further Reading

Maines, B., & Robinson, G. (2010). *The Support Group Method Training Pack: Effective Anti-bullying intervention*. Lucky Duck Books.

Robinson, G., & Maines, B. (2008). *Bullying: A Complete Guide to the Support Group Method*. Sage.

Rigby, K. (2013). *The 6 Methods of Intervention*, Department of Education and Early Childhood. www.education.vic.gov.au/Documents/about/programs/bullystoppers/krsupportgroup.pdf

11. THE METHOD OF SHARED CONCERN

This account is based upon suggestions made by Anatol Pikas (2002), the author of the method of shared concern, sometimes called the Pikas method. As with the support group method, this method is undertaken in cases of group bullying in which a number of perpetrators are thought to be involved.

The method involves several stages:

1. On the basis of reports or observations, identify and interview each of the suspected bullies one by one. Make no accusations, but share your concern about the person you believe is having a hard time at school. No need to mention bullying! Seek to gain the suspected bully's recognition of the person's plight as well as their unforced collaboration in finding a good solution.

2. After a few days, meet with each of the individual suspected bullies again quite briefly to ascertain what they have been able to do. Do not threaten anyone if their promises have not yet been fulfilled, but remind them of what they said.

3. Next, conduct an interview with the targeted student to find out how things are going. Offer your support. You may explain that you have talked with some students who know about what has been happening and that they have offered to help to improve the situation. Give assurances that no-one is going to be punished and it is safe to tell. Because *sometimes* the victim has provoked the bullying, it wise to explore this possibility, gently. Remember you need to gain the victim's confidence!

4. When you believe that some good progress has been made by the suspected bullies – and it usually it has – invite all of them to a meeting where the matter will be discussed further. Ask them to make a plan together – and rehearse what they will say at the next meeting when the target joins them.

5. Start the final meeting next day, if possible, with the victim sitting next to you, to be joined a little later by the group of suspected bullies. They each in turn make their agreed statement. It may be an apology. It may sometimes include a requirement that the victim must behave better, that is, if they have been provocative. The practitioner's role is to help them to reach a solution that is acceptable to all parties.

6. Finally, it is important to monitor what happens next. If there is any further problem, another meeting will be needed. Fortunately, the method has a very high level of success and often no further meeting is needed. An Australian Government-funded evaluation of this method has provided details of its use and reported effectiveness (see Rigby and Griffiths, 2011).

A cartoon version of the stages of the method is given on the next two pages. Discuss and clarify each of the stages.

1. The method can begin when a student is identified as being in some distress and it is believed that they are being bullied. Generally at this stage the student is *not* interviewed, but inquiries are made about who might be the perpetrators.

2. A group of students suspected of doing the bullying is identified. Each one of them is then interviewed separately to help the practitioner (the teacher) to understand what may be happening and to invite their assistance in improving the situation.

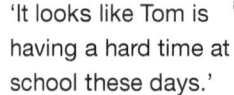

'It looks like Tom is having a hard time at school these days.'

3. In one-to-one situations with the suspected bullies, the practitioner shares a concern for the student who is in distress and seeks to gain their cooperation to improve the situation. No accusations are made. The practitioner asks how the student might help, and reinforces positive suggestions and commitments to act.

11. The method of shared concern

Source: Adapted from Rigby (n.d.-b)

After seeing each one of the suspected bullies, the bullied student is interviewed, offered support and informed that the students who have been giving them a hard time have actually offered to improve the situation in some way. The bullied student is asked tactfully whether they might have provoked the bullies. Assurance is given of continuing support, and arrangements are made for another meeting to review progress.

After each of the suspected bullies has been seen a second time to ascertain progress, a group meeting is called. At this the group members are praised individually for what they have done to help. They are then asked to discuss what they are prepared to say at the next meeting when the targeted student will attend. They rehearse what they will say.

A positive outcome commonly results as the suspected bullies and/or leader assures the target that they are sorry about what has happened and that the bullying will not continue. The targeted student may be reassured. However, the practitioner makes it clear that if there are further issues they will come together again.

Sometimes the process does not run so smoothly. The target may have acted provocatively. Hence, in this case, they need to convince the suspected bullies that they will change their behaviour. This needs to be done before a reconciliation can be achieved. The practitioner must act here as a mediator.

Preparation for using the method of shared concern

It is recommended that before applying this method some careful preparation is needed. It is very helpful to view *The Method of Shared Concern: A Staff Training Resource for Bullying*. This video illustrates how the method can be applied in working with a group of male and a group of female adolescents suspected of bullying a targeted peer. See www.readymade.com.au/method for a free preview of this resource, which can be purchased from the same site. Because it takes as long as an hour to view and should be discussed afterwards, it is suggested that an entire session be used for viewing and discussing the DVD.

Role-plays may be performed to enable potential users to prepare themselves further. Often the most important role-play is that in which a practitioner works with an individual member of a group who is suspected of bullying a particular victim. Ideally this should precede any interview with the victim, so that the practitioner gets to know the interviewees and seeks their cooperation without being in a position to make any accusations. However, quite often the victim has already approached the school and the bullies are already known! Nonetheless, practitioners should make no accusations but instead concentrate on the plight of the victim and the need for help from the students suspected of bullying. Be as non-judgemental as possible.

ROLE-PLAY OF THE METHOD OF SHARED CONCERN

Work in twos: one taking the part of the practitioner, the other the bully. Assume the practitioner is meeting the bully for the first time.

It is important for this exercise that you follow the script quite closely. It is intended to show how a good or ideal interview could occur. Later we can discuss what might be done if the bully is not so cooperative; for example, if they refuse to acknowledge that the victim needs to be helped or that they have any responsibility in trying to improve the situation. But for this exercise, simply go along with the following script, of which both role-players should have a copy.

Conduct the interview with the practitioner and the suspected bully sitting opposite to each other, as in the cartoon version set out on pages 26–27. If you wish, a third person may act as an observer and contribute impressions afterwards.

Note that, although the role-play may be conducted by just two volunteers, it is generally much better to have everyone involved in a number of simultaneous role-plays.

Role-play script

The practitioner and suspected bully use the same script in this exercise.

Practitioner	Suspected bully
Greet them in a friendly manner. Make no accusations.	
Identify the person you want to talk about – give a name.	Indicate that you do know who that person is.
Share your concern about the way they are actually behaving (e.g., being miserable, upset, absent from school) and add that they 'seem to be having a hard time'.	Acknowledge that things aren't so good for them. Say what you have noticed.
Ask the suspected bully to say what they like. What do you think may be happening to them? Prompt where necessary.	Say what you think about them. Suggest what may be a reason for them being upset. Include how others are treating them.
Listen carefully and non-critically. Then ask what they could do to improve the situation.	Make some suggestions (e.g., I will talk to them, ask my friends to leave them alone).
Reinforce everything positive and realistic the student may say, and confirm that they are really ready to do such things.	Indicate that you will carry out what you have suggested.
Thank the student warmly for their help and make arrangements for another meeting at an agreed time and place.	

On conclusion, share brief impressions of how the interview went from the points of view of the practitioner and the bully.

Next consider what might in practice happen in some interviews when cooperation does not occur. Consider alternatives: for example, arranging another meeting; using another practitioner; if all else fails, proceeding with the method without this person; and (if necessary) as a last resort, disciplinary action.

Further stages of the method of shared concern

Group discussion of the subsequent stages of the method should be undertaken. To do this it is best to examine again the cartoon version of the method given on pages 26–27.

Staff may wish to role-play the group meetings, including the last one in which mediation is attempted. Alternatively, the following questions can be simply discussed while viewing the cartooned version.

1. What if any of suspected bullies interviewed earlier refuse to attend the group meeting? Should disciplinary action be taken? What if the targeted student will not attend?
2. Should the targeted student be compelled to attend the final group meeting?
3. Is it *ever* fair to allow the group of bullies to make demands upon the target to change in some way before the bullying will cease?
4. Should the participants be asked to sign a contract indicating what they have agreed to do or not do?
5. Are group meetings really necessary if each suspected bully agrees to help in the first meeting?
6. Should the school follow up on what transpires after the final meeting?

The originator of the method, Anatol Pikas, would answer as follows:

1. Where there is a lack of cooperation on the part of the suspected bullies, then the school may reasonably decide that sanctions be applied. Fortunately, if this intervention is well applied, it is rare for this to happen.
2. If the targeted student does not wish to attend the meeting, as sometimes occurs, try to persuade, but do not compel attendance. (If close support is offered the target will generally come along.)
3. The bullies may sometimes be right in believing that the behaviour of the provocative victim is part of the problem and the victim may need to accept *some* responsibility.
4. If there is doubt about the bullies keeping their word, yes, employ a contract everybody present signs.
5. Group meetings are highly desirable, as the total group must be engaged with and make a collective and sustainable commitment.
6. Following up, as with other methods, is definitely required.

Further reading

Pikas, A. (2002). New developments in shared concern method. *School Psychology International*, 23(3), 307–336.

Rigby, K. (n.d.). How the method of shared concern works. *KenRigby.net*. www.kenrigby.net/11e-Shared-Concern-Method-How-it-Works

Rigby, K. (2009). School bullying and the case for the method of shared concern. In S. Jimerson, S. Swearer, & D. Espelage (Eds), *The International Handbook of School Bullying*, (pp. 547–558). Routledge.

Rigby, K. (2011). *The Method of Shared Concern: A Positive Approach to Bullying in Schools*. ACER.

Rigby, K., & Griffiths, C. (2011). Addressing cases of bullying through the method of shared concern. *School Psychology International*, *32*(3), 345–357.

12. OTHER INTERVENTION METHODS

Earlier it was noted that there are other potentially helpful methods of case intervention beyond the six interventions that have so far been highlighted. These include the following.

Solution-focused brief therapy (SFBT)

This approach involves the use of non-directive support being provided by a teacher or counsellor to the victim of bullying. In some respects, this is similar to the strengthening the victim approach (page 10); however, SFBT emphasises the importance of helping the student to recognise their potential strengths and how their employment could contribute to the solution of the problem. Examples and evaluations are given by Young and Haldorf (2003).

Discussion question

Do you think victims of bullying generally have the potential to solve the difficulties that they experience by being helped to recognise their strengths and recall the successes they have had in the past?

School tribunals or bully courts

Students are elected by their peers to hear evidence and recommend the use of appropriate sanctions or punishments for those identified as bullying someone. Mahdavi and Smith (2002) have provided a detailed description of this method of intervention operated in a secondary school in England and an assessment of its effectiveness.

Discussion question

Can students be trusted to elect responsible representatives who can make sound and acceptable judgements about cases of bullying? Is bullying a problem that should be addressed entirely by staff members?

Motivational interviewing

Students are invited, if they wish, to discuss with a teacher or counsellor any aspect of their behaviour that they feel is personally problematic, such as the habit of bullying others. In such a case, the student is assisted in exploring the pros and cons of the behaviour and the ramifications of any changes they may decide to make. See Cross et al. (2018) for more information about this method.

Discussion question

Under what circumstances (if any) might you expect students who have engaged in bullying at school to seek help from teachers about how they might change? Can teachers discuss the matter *without* directing students on how they *should* behave?

13. GROUP BULLYING AND BULLYING BY INDIVIDUAL STUDENTS

An important distinction has been made in this book between group bullying and bullying by individuals. It must, however, be acknowledged that distinguishing between group and individual bullying can, in practice, be difficult.

Some group involvement – as in bystanders supporting a bully – may occur in a school, and it is not always clear whether a person engaged in the act of bullying is doing so without the support, active or passive, of some peers. Research has shown that when victims of bullying are asked to say whether they have been bullied by an individual or a group, many say 'both'. Some identify only one person and some only a group.

Generally, being bullied by a group is more distressing than being bullied by an individual, and also more difficult to resolve. Where a group of suspected perpetrators is involved, the traditional use of sanctions is often unsuccessful, and sometimes unjust. Some members may be more culpable than others. In any case, if a group of students are collectively accused of bad behaviour, they are inclined to support each other and become very resistant to change.

Seeking to help students who are being bullied by a group by teaching them better social skills is often ineffective, especially if the bullying they are subjected to is motivated by social prejudice (as in racism and intolerance of sexual orientation or unusual physical appearance). The negative impact of name-calling and ostracism may be reduced by helping students to develop a stoical attitude to negative events, but the more realistic approach is to seek and apply means, ideally educational, that stop the bullying from continuing.

Education for change may come about through lessons that are part of the school curriculum. However, it can often be more effective for a teacher or counsellor to work closely with a group of perpetrators and the targeted student, or with students who offer social support – that is, by applying the support group method (page 22) or the method of shared concern (page 25).

14. CYBERBULLYING

Cyberbullying is sometimes classified as a crime, regardless of its severity. The police are to be informed and legal action may follow. Where this is the case, alternative methods of intervention by schools may be unacceptable.

However, once a school has been alerted to a case of cyberbullying and is aware of the student or students involved, they may choose to investigate further. In most cases, the students in question are also engaging in traditional forms of bullying for which the methods described in this booklet may be appropriate. For instance, if the students sending offensive or threatening messages to someone can be identified as bullying in other ways at school, the support group method (page 22) or the method of shared concern (page 25) may be helpful in stopping the bullying and improving relationships. Restorative practices (page 19) may be employed to help offenders to appreciate the harm they have done and thereby stop bullying by all means.

It should be understood that cyberbullying is generally an extension of traditional forms of bullying practices at school and is, like all bullying, a systematic abuse of power for which there are various possible remedies.

Sometimes it is unclear whether cyberbullying is being conducted by students at the same school as the victim and whether the school has any responsibility in taking any action. Whatever the case may be, it is advisable for parents to notify the school, as the school may decide to investigate further.

Further reading

Gabrielli. S., Rizzi. S., Carbone. S., & Piras, E. M. (2021). School interventions for bullying-cyberbullying prevention in adolescents: Insights from the UPRIGHT and CREEP Projects. *International Journal of Environmental Research and Public Health*, *18*(21), 11697.

15. Choosing the Best Methods

1. First, there must be agreement about whether, under each circumstance, a particular intervention method *can* be applied at your school.
2. Practitioners of any method of intervention require a good understanding of how it can be applied. Some instruction and training should be made available.
3. When actions on the part of perpetrators are regarded as criminal, as in physical assaults and (in some jurisdictions) cyberbullying, the use of appropriate legal sanctions is definitely required.
4. Sanctions applied by a school should be proportionate in severity to the seriousness of the offence. They are more likely to be effective if sanctions are seen by students as justified, it is understood that future behaviour will be rigorously monitored and, if satisfactory, their bullying behaviour will not be held against them.
5. Whether a case of bullying can be addressed and prevented from continuing by providing training for a student in appropriate social skills, as fogging (page 10), is a matter for considered judgement – and in some circumstances it may not be realistic.
6. Mediation should not be forced upon students, but it may be applied under some circumstances when students themselves want help in resolving a relationship problem that could involve conflict or lead to bullying.
7. Restorative practices are generally practicable when a bully can be brought to appreciate the harm that has been done and expresses sincere remorse, without being stigmatised. If this cannot be achieved, an alternative approach will be needed.
8. Where group bullying takes place, one may consider the use of either the support group method (page 22) or the method of shared concern (page 25).
9. The success of the support group method (page 22) depends largely on whether assistance can be obtained from pro-social students.

15. Choosing the best methods

10. The success of the method of shared concern (page 25) depends on:
    a. the positive relationship achieved through one-to-one interviews, together with a commitment to help resolve the problem
    b. subsequently enabling the group of bullies and the person they have targeted to work out and 'own' an agreed solution
    c. close monitoring of the outcome.
11. The method of shared concern is the *only* method that seeks to provide a solution to a problem in which the victim has in fact acted provocatively, as happens in a significant minority of cases.
12. Whatever the method or combination of intervention methods actually employed, gaining the confidence and collaboration of parents is needed.
13. Whatever intervention is undertaken it should be consistent with the school's anti-bullying policy.
14. The method of intervention employed should be accurately recorded and the outcomes monitored (see Appendix B).

16. EXERCISE ON SELECTING A METHOD

As an aid to discussing what choices may be made in the employment of a given method, teachers may like to consider the following cases and decide which method or methods may be most appropriate for dealing with each case.

The methods to choose from are: (A) the traditional disciplinary approach, (B) strengthening the victim, (C) mediation, (D) restorative practice, (E) the support group method, (F) the method of shared concern, (G) solution-focused brief therapy, (H) school tribunals or bully courts, and (I) motivational interviewing.

Next to each of the cases given on the coming pages, note the most appropriate method or methods of intervention using the corresponding letter(s). Remember, *more than one method* may be appropriate to apply in a single case of bullying; for example, (A) the traditional disciplinary approach *and* (B) strengthening the victim.

There are no absolutely correct answers. What is wanted is your opinion.

> **Case 1:** A thirteen-year-old boy has been hospitalised as a result of being physically assaulted by another student.
>
> **Case 2:** Several girls in secondary school have been identified as spreading rumours about another girl's sexual orientation. The subject of the rumour is very angry about it.
>
> **Case 3:** Several boys in a group have been making lewd remarks with sexual innuendo in the presence of a girl who has become upset by their behaviour.
>
> **Case 4:** A quiet, shy, nine-year-old girl is being ridiculed by some girls in her class. She has started staying away from school. She tells the teacher about how upset she is.
>
> **Case 5:** A twelve-year-old girl has been continually targeted by a group of students who make fun of her disability. There are other students in her class who think this is unfair.
>
> **Case 6:** Two nine-year-old boys have been observed as continually arguing and upsetting each other at school. Both boys would like the quarrelling to stop.

Case 7: *A particularly robust six-year-old boy has been observed continually pushing around and upsetting other less powerful children. Despite repeated assurances that he would stop, the bullying continues.*

Case 8: *A fifteen-year-old female student has been identified as the sender of offensive and threatening cyber messages to her former friend. It is suggested that the police be notified; however, the target of the attacks and her parents are open to an alternative resolution.*

Case 9: *A boy in secondary school has been identified as continually upsetting another younger boy by taunting him about his father being in jail. When asked to reflect on what he has been doing, the older boy feels ashamed of himself.*

Case 10: *A fifteen-year-old girl is troubled about how she is being regarded by other students, who describe her as bossy and insensitive. She is wondering whether she should make an effort to change the way she has been relating to others.*

When complete, members of the group may be asked to share their judgements. Be prepared to give reasons for your choice and if uncertain say what further information you would need to decide.

As a supplementary exercise, teachers may like to describe a recent case of bullying that was identified and addressed at their school, and discuss whether it might have been addressed differently in light of what has been learned in this workshop.

Further reading

See 'Chapter 11: Choosing a method' in the following:

Rigby, K. (2010). *Bullying Interventions in Schools: Six Basic Approaches*. ACER.

17. INTERVIEWING STUDENTS INVOLVED IN BULLYING

A major difficulty in addressing bullying can be accessing victims. Research has shown that a high proportion of students who have been bullied do not want to tell a teacher – whether that is because they regard the bullying as something they can live with, because they do not think that teachers could or would help, or because teachers would probably make matters worse. Bystanders are often averse to informing or 'dobbing' on other students. It follows that teachers may have to demonstrate a capacity to help, and students need to be convinced that teachers are not only concerned with the acquisition of knowledge and the imposition of discipline, but that they also have a genuine interest in how vulnerable students are being treated by others.

While talking with and interviewing students, individually and collectively, is an everyday practice for teachers, working with people who are most relevant to cases of bullying may constitute challenges that are not present on most occasions. This includes interviewing students who have been identified as bullying someone, individually or in a group; those who have been victimised; bystanders (if any); and the parents of suspected victims and bullies.

As explained earlier in this book, the method employed by a teacher or counsellor may vary according to the kind of case. They may also require interview skills that are appropriate for one-to-one meetings, group meetings or both, as in the method of shared concern (page 25). In addition, the general orientation of a teacher may influence the way they interact with identified victims or bullies. According to research into the moral orientations of teachers, some emphasise the need for justice, while others emphasise the need for care. Both can be important.

The natural inclination of most people is to blame the bully. (A small minority blame the victim and may even argue that bullying provides appropriate feedback for students who need it.) A strong disposition to blame can result in a student being misunderstood, as when bullying has been provoked. Sometimes with non-violent bullying a bully may be brought to really understand that they have an obligation to remedy the situation, and this possibility opens the way to a positive solution.

Understanding why people behave as they do usually requires careful and non-judgemental listening to what they say. Here is a counsel of perfection proposed by the nineteenth-century Danish existential philosopher Søren Kierkegaard:

> Surely, I must understand what he understands. If I do not know that, my greater understanding will be of no help to him. If however, I am disposed to plume myself on my greater understanding it is because I am vain or proud, so that at bottom, instead of benefitting him, I want to be admired. But all true effort to help begins with self-humiliation: the helper must first humble himself under him he would help, and therewith must understand that to help does not mean to be sovereign but to be a servant, that to help does not mean to be ambitious but to be patient; that to help means to endure for the time being the imputation that one is in the wrong and does not understand what the other understands.
> (as cited in Bretall, 1946, pp. 333–334)

Insofar as one can approach this ideal, an understanding of the situation becomes clearer and may help to guide what needs to be done. The philosophy underlying the need to listen attentively to children suspected of bullying is explored further in Rigby (2021a).

Working with parents of those identified as bullies or as victims may present further challenges. Typically, parents of children who are being bullied welcome the assistance offered by the school; indeed, they are generally the ones who have sought and initiated the meeting. Research based on student responses to surveys indicate that bullied children are more likely to inform their parents than teachers.

Difficulties can arise when parents believe that the school has been culpable in not recognising that their child is being bullied and in proposing solutions that are not acceptable. Parents are inclined to favour the traditional use of punishment and insist that the parents of the bully must be contacted. Schools sometimes choose a different approach, depending largely on the severity of the bullying and their knowledge of alternative courses of action. Understandably, they are often not prepared to say what they will do, beyond saying they will investigate further.

Parents often want to be informed about whatever the school has done. Given that schools are not bound to disclose everything they do about a bullying incident, conflict can arise, and this can require considerable diplomacy and patience. Keeping in touch with parents about the bullying behaviour is something that schools are obligated to do. Some schools go further and counsel parents on how they might provide emotional support for their children and help them to develop more adequate social skills.

Interviewing the parents of children who have been identified as bullies can be quite confronting. Care must be taken to not make claims about what the bully has done without clear evidence: for instance, that which is obtained from direct observation or from reliable witnesses. It is best to avoid accusations or any suggestion that the parents are to blame. The parents sometimes seek to justify their child's aggressive acts – and in some cases it should be recognised that there had been a degree of provocation. The school, however, needs to stand firm and address the unacceptability of the behaviour, without ever impugning the character of the child or a parent. Again, the school may usefully suggest assistance in improving the child's behaviour: for example, through training in anger management, if appropriate, and even in mindfulness.

The question is sometimes raised as to whether the parents of the bully and the parents of the victim should meet to resolve the problem. There have been occasions on which such meetings have led to a serious escalation, and this approach is commonly discouraged. At the same time, some parents have reported positive outcomes. It depends very much on the prior relationship (if any) between the parents involved. A positive solution is more likely if there is a good mediator present.

In working with groups of students who are, or have been, bullying someone, is it possible for them to be brought to a realisation that there is a better way of behaving? This is, of course, the ideal outcome. Traditionally this has been attempted largely through religious instruction. There are other means. For instance, through the method of shared concern (page 25) change can be brought about through a recognition in a group of a better way for which they are themselves responsible. There is a Russian proverb that Pikas remarked upon in conversation with me: 'All children between one and one hundred years adopt an idea if they discover it as their own.' If this can be achieved, we really have a durable solution.

18. THE SCHOOL ANTI-BULLYING POLICY AND ITS RELATIONSHIP WITH DEALING WITH CASES OF BULLYING

An anti-bullying policy is a document, generally required by education authorities, containing guidelines that schools are expected to follow in addressing bullying. A description of the basic elements of a school anti-bullying policy is available online at www.kenrigby.net/05-elements-of-a-school-antibullying-policy

A school's anti-bullying policy needs to encapsulate what that school pledges to do to counter bullying, both preventively and through educational input in classrooms, providing a positive supportive ethos for everyone in the school community, and through close collaboration with parents. It needs to begin with a statement of accepted values. It needs to recognise the seriousness of countering bullying behaviour. Rather than being a dry, formal and bureaucratic document, it should act not only as a guide to what is to be done; it should also be inspirational. It should be made available to and discussed by all parents and guardians, and most importantly students. (It is unfortunately the case that many students report that they are unaware whether the school has such a policy.)

How a school will address actual cases of bullying is *one* important part of such a document. Sometimes I see statements that the school will take decisive action based on the professional experience of teachers in dealing with such issues. This is practically non-informative and of little or no value to teachers, parents or lawyers. As far as possible the policy on case interventions should include *brief* accounts of specific strategies the school may employ. Teachers or counsellors should have relevant know-how about and agreement on the use of these strategies.

On the following page you will find some suggestions about what *could* be included. Go through them point by point and obtain a high level of agreement on whether each should ever be used and under what circumstances.

- Members of the school community (including students, teachers and parents) are required to report any cases of bullying that they believe should be handled by the school.
- Every reported case will be examined and appropriate actions taken.
- Action may include the following:
    i. the use of sanctions or consequences for the bully
    ii. providing help and support to the student who has been bullied
    iii. mediation between students who are in conflict and request assistance in overcoming a problem
    iv. the use of restorative practices whereby the bully or bullies are required to recognise the harm they have done and make amends
    v. obtaining active support from selected pro-social students who can meet with the identified bullies, together with a staff member, to assist and improve the situation for the targeted student (as in the support group method)
    vi. identifying and meeting first with *individuals* who are part of a group engaged in bullying someone, sharing a concern for the victim, and subsequently requiring that they all meet together with a staff member *and* the victim to work out how they will put things right (as in the method of shared concern)
    vii. consultation with students regarding their views on what actions by the school are appropriate in given cases.

    It is reasonable to indicate that one or a combination of these actions may be taken, as considered appropriate. (The school is not committed to any particular method of intervention, but rather is asserting that there are methods it *may* use, depending on the circumstances.)
- In all cases parents will be consulted and informed about actions that have been taken by the school.
- Police will be informed in cases of physically violent assault.
- The effects of every intervention will be monitored by the school and, if necessary, further action taken.

Finally, improving a school's capacity to handle cases of bullying is a long-term project. Decisions about the best ways of dealing with particular cases of bullying can change over time with experience. The records that can be kept (as supported by the form given in Appendix B, pages 46–49) can be a valuable source of information as to what changes and consequent modifications to school anti-bullying policies are needed.

APPENDIX A: OUTCOMES

TABLE 1: Outcomes of interventions in cases of bullying as reported by students, schools and parents

	Studies	Stopped (%)	Reduced (%)	No change (%)	Worsened (%)
Student reports	Smith & Shu, 2000 (England)	26	29	28	16
	Rigby, 1998 (Australia)	49		43	8
	Rigby & Barnes, 2002 (Australia)	42		39	18
	Fekkes et al., 2005 (Netherlands)	49		34	17
	Davis & Nixon, 2011 (United States)	34		37	29
	Rigby and Johnson, 2016 (Australia)	29	40	23	8
	Wachs et al., 2019 (Germany)	22	44	30	4
School reports	Thompson & Smith, 2011 (England)	67	20	13	
	Girandeau et al., 2014 (Finland)	78	20	2	0
	Rigby & Johnson, 2016 (Australia)	78		19	4
Parent reports	Rigby & Johnson, 2016 (Australia)	27	33	30	10

Note: Percentages may not total 100 due to rounding. Figures in the boxes are combined categories only, as in 'bullying stopped' and 'bullying reduced', and for 'bullying reduced' and 'bullying worsened.' The findings reported by Wachs et al. (2019) are based on reports provided by a sample of students that included some who were not victims of bullying: for example, bystanders of the bullying incidents; other student reports were from self-reports of victims.

APPENDIX B: RECORDING FORM

This recording form (downloadable and reproducible) is for use by staff members to record information relating to an incident or episode of bullying that led to the school taking action. It must be filed securely and made available to the school principal in any review of the case.

BACKGROUND TO THE BULLYING

1. When did the bullying take place? Over what period?

2. Where did it happen?

3. Who was engaged in doing the bullying? *(Tick as relevant, give names.)*
   - ☐ One boy
   - ☐ One girl
   - ☐ Several boys
   - ☐ Several girls
   - ☐ Both boys and girls
   - ☐ Other

4. Who was bullied? Give name, age, gender and any other characteristics that appear relevant (e.g., ethnicity, disability etc.).

5. How did you learn about the bullying? *(Tick one or more.)*
   - ☐ The victim came for help.
   - ☐ A staff member observed the bullying.
   - ☐ The bullying was reported by another student or students.
   - ☐ A parent informed the school.

   Add any other source of information about the bullying:

Appendix B: Recording form

6. What form did the bullying take? *(Tick one or more.)*
    - ☐ Physical
    - ☐ Verbal
    - ☐ Exclusion or rumour spreading
    - ☐ Cyberbullying
    - ☐ Other *(add)* _____

7. How was the victim affected? *(Tick one or more.)*
    - ☐ The victim was physically hurt or injured.
    - ☐ The victim was seriously impacted emotionally (e.g., becoming very upset, depressed, frightened).
    - ☐ The victim stayed away from school because of the bullying.
    - ☐ The bullying made it hard for the victim to do their schoolwork well.

8. How severe or serious do you think the bullying was? *(Tick one only.)*
    - ☐ Of minor concern
    - ☐ Quite serious
    - ☐ Very serious

9. How long has the bullying been going on?

   _____

ACTION TAKEN BY THE SCHOOL

Were the following actions undertaken? *(Tick all that were undertaken.)*

- ☐ One or more persons who had observed the bullying was interviewed
- ☐ The bully or bullies were confronted by a staff member.
- ☐ The parent or parents of the bully or bullies were spoken with.
- ☐ The parent or parents of the victim were spoken with.
- ☐ The bully or bullies were sanctioned or punished. If so, describe in what way:

_____

_____

_____

_____

Reproducible

- ☐ The victim was supported and advised on how to cope better with the situation. Who provided this help?

  ....

- ☐ Was any *training* provided for the victim (e.g., in responding to bullying behaviour)? If so, briefly describe what was done:

  ....

  ....

- ☐ A restorative practice was applied; that is, the bully and the victim were brought together at a meeting and the bully was required to appreciate and acknowledge the harm that had been done, apologise to the victim and restore acceptable relations.

- ☐ The support group method was used; that is, some students not involved in the bullying attended a meeting together with the identified bullies, and each person present was asked how they would act to improve the situation. Outcomes were then closely monitored.

- ☐ The method of shared concern was applied. *(Tick if each of the following was done.)*

  - ☐ Each of the suspected or known bullies was interviewed individually. The practitioner shared a concern for the victim's plight and the interviewee was invited to help to improve the situation.

  - ☐ Subsequently, the victim was interviewed, told of what had so far happened, given strong support and offered help to stop the bullying.

  - ☐ The victim was also asked to think about how they might possibly have provoked the bullying – but in no way blamed!

  - ☐ A meeting was held including all the suspected bullies to make plans on how to help further and prepare them to meet the person they had bullied.

  - ☐ A further meeting was held with the victim present. The suspected bullies indicated what they could do to improve relations and discontinue any bullying, and the victim was asked to consider their offer.

  - ☐ An agreement was reached among all the students involved about how they would henceforth treat the person they had bullied.

Appendix B: Recording form

☐ A contract was signed by all present to confirm the agreement, and the situation was monitored with the understanding that any breakdown would result in the school taking further action.

Add any further information about the intervention (e.g., referral to the police, outside counselling):

....
....

EVALUATING THE OUTCOME

1. Was the case followed up to discover whether the bullying had stopped? If so, with whom? *(Tick one or more.)*

   ☐ The victim

   ☐ The parents or guardians of the victim

   ☐ The bully or bullies

   ☐ The parents or guardians of the bully or bullies

   ☐ Others (e.g., students and teachers)

2. What was the outcome of the intervention?

   ☐ The bullying stopped

   ☐ The bullying reduced but did not stop

   ☐ There was no change

   ☐ The bullying got worse

   ☐ I don't know

3. Please add anything further that you think may be useful in evaluating what was done in this case, and any recommendations for the future:

....
....
....
....
....

Name and signature of teacher or counsellor completing this record:

....

Date: ....

Reproducible

REFERENCES AND RECOMMENDATIONS

Note: References preceded by an asterisk are recommended reading in preparation for workshops.

*Bauman, S., Rigby, K., & Hoppa, K. (2008). US teachers' and school counsellors' strategies for handling school bullying incidents. *Educational Psychology*, 28(7), 837–856.

Bretall, R. (Ed.) (1946). *Kierkegaard Anthology*. Princeton University Press.

Davis, S., & Nixon, C. (2011). What students say about bullying. *Educational Leadership*, 69(1), 18–23.

Fekkes, M., Pjipers, F. I. M., & Verloove-Vanhorick, S.P. (2005). Bullying: Who does what, when and where? Involvement of children, teachers and parents in bullying behavior. *Health Education Research*, 20(1), 81–91.

Garandeau, C. F., Poskiparta, E., & Salmivalli, C. (2014). Tackling acute cases of school bullying in the KiVa anti-bullying program: A comparison of two approaches. *Journal of Abnormal Child Psychology*, 42(6), 981–991.

Murphy, E., & Lewers, R. (2000). *The Hidden Hurt*. Wizard Books.

Readymade productions (n.d.). *The Method of Shared Concern: A Staff Training Resource for Bullying*. http://readymade.com.au/method

Rigby, K. (n.d.-a). Elements of a school anti-bullying policy. *KenRigby.net*. www.kenrigby.net/05-elements-of-a-school-antibullying-policy

Rigby, K. (n.d.-b). How the method of shared concern works. *KenRigby.net*. www.kenrigby.net/11e-Shared-Concern-Method-How-it-Works

Rigby, K. (1998). *Manual for the Peer Relations Questionnaire*. Professional Reading Guide.

Rigby, K. (2003). Consequences of Bullying in Schools. *The Canadian Journal of Psychiatry*, 48(9), 583–590.

Rigby, K. (2007). *Bullying in Schools and What to Do About It – Revised and Updated*. ACER.

*Rigby, K. (2010). *Bullying Interventions in Schools: Six Basic Approaches*. ACER.

Rigby, K. (2011a). *The Method of Shared Concern: A Positive Approach to Bullying*. ACER.

Rigby, K. (2011b). What can schools do about cases of bullying? *Pastoral Care in Education*, 29(4), 273–285.

Rigby, K. (2013). *The 6 Methods of Intervention*, Department of Education and Early Childhood. www.education.vic.gov.au/Documents/about/programs/bullystoppers/krsupportgroup.pdf

*Rigby, K. (2013). Bullying interventions. *Every Child Journal*, 3.5, 70–75.

Rigby, K. (2014) How teachers address cases of bullying in schools: A comparison of five reactive approaches. *Educational Psychology in Practice*, 30(4), 409–419.

Rigby, K. (2021a). Addressing cases of bullying in schools: Reactive strategies. In P. K. Smith & J. O'Higgins Norman (Eds.). *The Wiley Blackwell Handbook of Bullying: A Comprehensive and International Review of Research and Intervention* (Vol. 2, pp. 370–386). Wiley-Blackwell.

Rigby, K. (2021b). *Multi-perspectivity on Bullying in Schools: One Pair of Eyes is Not Enough*. Routledge.

Rigby, K., & Barnes, A. (2002). The victimised student's dilemma: To tell or not to tell. *Youth Studies Australia*, 21(3), 33–36.

Rigby, K., & Griffiths, C. (2011). Addressing cases of bullying through the method of shared concern. *School Psychology International*, 32(3), 345–357.

*Rigby, K. & Johnson, K. (2016.) *The prevalence and effectiveness of anti-bullying strategies employed in Australian schools*. University of South Australia.

Salmivalli, C., Kaukiainen, A., & Voeten, M. (2005) Anti-bullying intervention: Implementation and outcomes. *The British Journal of Educational Psychology*, 75(3), 465–487.

Sherer, Y. C., & Nickerson, A. B. (2010). Anti-bullying practices in American schools: Perspectives of school psychologists. *Psychology in the Schools*, 47(3), 217–229.

*Smith, P.K. (2014). *Understanding School Bullying: Its Nature & Prevention Strategies*. Sage.

Smith, P. K., Howard, S., & Thompson, F. (2007). Use of the support group method to tackle bullying, and evaluation from schools and local authorities in England. *Pastoral Care in Education*, 25(2), 4–13

Smith, P. K., Pepler, D., & Rigby, K. (2004). *Bullying in Schools: How Successful Can Interventions Be?* Cambridge University Press.

Smith, P. K. & Shu, S. (2000). What good schools can do about bullying: Findings from a survey in English schools after a decade of research and action. *Childhood*, 7(2), 193–212.

Thompson, F., & Smith, P. K. (2011). *The Use and Effectiveness of Anti-Bullying Strategies in Schools*. Research Report DFE-RR098. Department for Education.

Ttofi, M. M., & Farrington, D. P. (2011). Effectiveness of school-based programs to reduce bullying: A systematic and meta-analytic review. *Journal of Experimental Criminology*, 7, 27–56.

Wachs, S., Bilz, L., Niproschke, S., & Schubarth, W. (2019). Bullying intervention in schools: A multilevel analysis of teachers' success in handling bullying from the students' perspective. *The Journal of Early Adolescence*, 39(5), 642–668.

Wicking, A., & Rigby, K. (2021). *No Bullying: A Bullying Prevention Manual for Principals and Teachers*. Resilient Youth.

Further reading

A complete list of the author's publications on bullying can be found on his website:

Rigby, K. (n.d.). Publications. *KenRigby.net*. www.kenrigby.net/15-Publications

An account of the author's work in countering bullying in schools is contained in his autobiography:

Rigby, K (2023). *Oddly Enough: The Autobiography of Ken Rigby*. Green Hill Publishing.

www.ingramcontent.com/pod-product-compliance
Lightning Source LLC
Chambersburg PA
CBHW051319110526
44590CB00031B/4407